Sukoon-e-Shayari

Zindagi, Yaadein aur Kuch Ehsaas

Anita Poonia

BookLeaf Publishing
India | USA | UK

Made with ❤ on the BookLeaf Publishing Platform
www.bookleafpub.in
www.bookleafpub.com

Dedication

Un apno ke naam,
jin ke saath zindagi sukoon lagti hai,

meri beti ki nanhi si muskaan ke naam,
jisne bina lafzon ko samjhe bhi
mere naam ki ek kitaab ka sapna dekha,

aur mere humsafar ke naam,
jisne mere jazbaaton par bharosa kiya,
mujhe likhne ki himmat di,
aur in lafzon ko duniya tak pahunchane ka hausla diya.

Un doston ke naam bhi,
jo peeche chhoot gaye,
par har pal dil mein rehte hain,

aur un lamhon ke naam,
jinhe lafzon mein sametna zaroori tha.

(Dedicated to those loved ones with whom life feels peaceful, to my daughter's little smile, who, without yet understanding these poems, dreamed of seeing a book with my name on it, and to my life partner, who believed

in my emotions, gave me the courage to write, and inspired me to share these words with the world.

Also dedicated to those friends we left behind along the way, yet live in my heart every day, and to those moments that deserved to be captured in words.)

Preface

Yeh kitab kisi kahani ka panna nahi hai, balki zindagi ke un lamhon ka sangrah hai
jo aksar hum mehsoos toh karte hain, par keh nahi paate.
Bachpan ki narm yaadein, dosti ka bharosa, rozmarra ki zindagi ki thakaan,
aur pyaar ke woh ehsaas jo bina shor ke dil mein bas jaate hain -----
yeh sab milkar *Sukoon-e-Shayari* ban gaye.

Yeh shayari kisi ko samjhaane ke liye nahi likhi gayi,
na hi kisi jawaab ki talaash mein hai.
Yeh bas ek koshish hai --- thahar kar mehsoos karne ki,
khud se milne ki, aur un ehsaason ko lafzon mein baandhne ki, jo kahin na kahin hum sab ke apne se lagte hain.

Agar in alfaazon mein aapko apni koi yaad, koi muskurahat,
ya bas ek pal ka sukoon mil jaaye, toh yeh shayari apna kaam kar gayi.

(This book is not any chapter of a story, but a collection of moments from life—
moments we often feel deeply, yet struggle to put into words.
The softness of childhood memories, the comfort of friendships, the exhaustion of everyday life,
and the quiet emotions of love that settle gently in the heart ---- together, they form Sukoon-e-Shayari.

These poems are not written to explain anything, nor to search for answers.
They are simply an attempt to pause, to feel, to reconnect with oneself, and to give words to emotions that, in some way, belong to all of us.
If these verses bring back a memory, a smile, or even a brief moment of calm, then this poetry has found its purpose.)

Acknowledgements

Yeh pustak un apno ki den hai,
jo har mod par mujhe sambhaalte rahe,
un alfaazon ki himmat hai,
jo mere dil se nikal kar
aage badhte rahe.

Un sabhi ka dil se shukriya,
jo is safar mein mere rahi bane,
mere khamosh jazbaaton ko samjha,
aur jab main thaki ya ruk gayi,
mujhe phir se chalna sikha gaye.

(This book is the result of countless moments of encouragement, belief, and support that guided me forward.
I am deeply grateful to everyone who stood by me during this journey - who listened to my words, motivated me through moments of doubt, and reminded me to keep moving ahead.

This book would not have been possible without your love and support.)

1. Bachpan (Childhood)

Bachpan ki vo hansi, masti se bhari vo baatein
(That laughter of childhood, those conversations filled with mischief and joy)
Khelte khelte hi jaise, guzar jaati thi saari raatein
(As if entire nights slipped away while we were lost in play)

Vo garmi ki chuttiyon mein, doston sang din bitana
(Those summer vacations, spending endless days with friends)
Na koi chinta thi, na gham ka koi bahana
(There were no worries, no excuses for sadness)

Sitaron mein apne khwabon ko khojna,
(Searching our dreams among the stars,)
Khuli chhat pe vo sitaron ke neeche sona
(Sleeping under the open sky, beneath a blanket of stars)

Dadi, nani ki kahaniyan,
(Stories told by grandma,)
Sone se pehle lori ban kar aana
(Turning into lullabies before sleep arrived)

Chhoti chhoti shabaashiyon mein,
(In small words of praise,)
chhupa tha poora jahaan
(an entire world felt complete)
Har pal mein khushi chhupi thi,
(Every moment held happiness,)
aur har hansi mein poora jeevan
(and every smile carried a whole life)

2. Bachpan laut aaye (May childhood return)

Kya tumhe yaad hai
(Do you remember,)
pehli baarish mein kagaz ki naav banana,
(making paper boats in the very first rain,)
mitti se sane, kichad mein lathpath ghar laut aana.
(covered in mud, soaked in slush, finding our way back home.)

Maa ka daantna,
(Mother's scolding,)
aur phir bhi apni masti mein khoye rehna,
(and yet, remaining lost in our own fun,)
kitna befikar sa tha vo bachpan.
(how carefree it all felt in childhood.)

Na logon ki soch ki parwah,
(no worry about what people might think,)
na sawaalon ka koi dar,
(no fear of questions or judgments,)
bas khel, dost, khana, aur apni hi dhun mein jhumna.
(just play, friends, food, and living freely in our own rhythm.)

Kaash... vo din, vo sacchi hansi,
(If only...those lighter days, those honest smiles,)
vo bachpan ek baar phir laut aaye.
(that childhood could return once again.)

3. Sukoon bhara bachpan (Innocent childhood)

Bachpan me zindagi kitni sukoon bhari thi,
(How innocent life was when we were young,)
har baat mein sacchai thi,
(there was honesty in every word,)
chehre pe koi naqaab nhi,
(no masks on our faces,)
bas ek masoomiyat hoti thi.
(only a pure, simple innocence.)

Na kisi ka dil dukhana jaante the,
(We did not know how to hurt anyone,)
na dil mein nafrat ka bojh tha,
(there was no weight of hatred in our hearts,)
na jhooth bolne ki aadat thi,
(no habit of lying,)
na kisi se chhupne ka dar
(nor the fear of hiding from someone.)

Sab ki khushiyon mein khul kar hans lete the,
(In everyone's happiness, we laughed freely,)
aur jab aankhen bhar aati thi,
(and when our eyes filled with tears,)
to bina jhijhak sab ke saamne ro lete the.

(without any hesitation, we cried openly before everyone.)

Na duniya ko samajhne ki jaldi thi,
(There was no hurry to understand the world,)
na khud ko chhupane ki zarurat,
(no need to hide who we were,)
kitne sukoon se guzarti thi zindagi
(how peacefully life passed by)
jab hum chhote the.
(when we were young.)

4. Maa ki god (In a mother's embrace)

Maa ki god mein, na jaane kya ehsaas hota hai,
(In a mother's embrace, there is an indescribable feeling,)
kitni bhi ho pareshani, uski baahon mein
(no matter how many worries there are, within her arms)
ek gehra sa sukoon hota hai.
(there is a deep, quiet peace.)

Maa ki mamta ka woh aanchal,
(That nurturing shade of a mother's love,)
uske haathon ka woh sparsh,
(the gentle touch of her hands,)
thakaan bhare din ke baad
(after a day filled with exhaustion,)
jaise mil jaaye khud se milne ka arsh.
(feels like meeting oneself again.)

Chahe kitne hi gham kyun na ho,
(No matter how many sorrows there are,)
maa ki ek muskaan,
(a single smile from a mother)
sab kuch halka kar deti hai,
(makes everything feel lighter,)
uski baaton mein hain aisa sukoon

(in her words there is such calm)

jo har pal ko,

(that makes every moment)

khushiyon se bhar deti hai.

(filled with happiness.)

5. School ke din (World outside home begins)

Kya tumhe yaad hain woh school ke din,
(Do you remember those school days,)
woh naye-naye dost banana,
(making new friends,)
sab ke saath khana baant kar khana.
(sharing food with everyone.)

Tiffin khulne se pehle hi bhookh ka badh jaana,
(Feeling hungry even before the tiffin was opened, hunger growing impatient,)
aur chup-chup kar class mein gappe maarna.
(and chatting inside the classroom.)

Homework ka darr, recess ki ghanti ka intezaar,
(The fear of homework, waiting eagerly for the recess bell,)
teacher ki nazar se bachna,
(escaping the teacher's watchful eyes,)
aur doston ke saath har pal ko khaas bana lena.
(and with friends turning every moment into something special.)

Woh din bhi kya din the,
(Those truly were special days,)
jab zimmedaariyon ka bojh nahi tha,
(when there was no weight of responsibility,)
sirf school ka bag kandhon par,
(only a school bag on our shoulders,)
aur doston ka saath dil ke paas tha.
(and the warmth of friendship close to our hearts.)

6. Tyohar aur bachpan (Festivals and childhood)

Bachpan me tyohar ka matlab sirf tareekh nahi hota tha,
(Festivals did not mean just a date on the calendar in childhood,)
woh ek intezaar hota tha,
(they were a feeling of anticipation.)

Naye kapdon ki khushboo, maa ke naye naye pakwan
(The fragrance of new clothes, something special preparedby a mother's hands,)
ghar ka shor aur hansi mein din ka beet jaana.
(the liveliness of the home and days passing wrapped in laughter.)

Diye, rang, aur chhoti si khushi,
(Lamps, colours, and simple joys,)
har tyohar apne saath yaadein chhod jaata tha.
(every festival left behind memories to be cherished.)

Woh tyohar bhi kya tyohar the,
(Those festivals were truly special,)
jab sab saath hote the,
(when togetherness was enough,)

aur bachpan ke sang
(and with childhood by our side,)
har Khushi poori lagti thi.
(every happiness felt complete.)

7. Bachpan badal gaya hai (Childhood has changed)

Kuch aisa lagta hai
(It feels as though)
ki bachpan ka matlab badal gaya hai,
(the meaning of childhood has changed,)
aaj ke daur mein sirf insaan hi nahi,
(in today's times, not just people,)
bachpana bhi badal gaya hai.
(but childhood itself has changed.)

Woh aankhon ki masoomiyat, kahin kho si gayi hai,
(That innocence that once lived in young eyes, seems to have faded away,)
bachche aaj bhi chillaate hain,
(children still laugh and shout today,)
par unki masum shararatein, kahin peeche chhoot gayi hain
(but their pure mischief feels like it has been left behind.)

Garmi ki chhuttiyan ab bhi aati hain,
(Summer vacations still come every year,)
par khelne ka woh junoon
(but the passion for play)
jaise kho sa gaya hai,

(seems to have quietly gone,)
naani ki kahaniyan, daadi ki loriyan ---
(grandmother's stories and lullabies---)
yeh sab ab phone me simat gaya hai.
(all of it now lives mostly in phone.)

Ab bachpan bhi ek daud ban gaya hai,
(Now even childhood has turned into a race,)
seekhne ki is hod mein, bachpan badal gaya hai
(in this rush to learn and achieve, childhood has changed.)

8. Dosti (Friendship)

Dosti ek aisa ahsas hai,
(Friendship is a feeling)
jo har pal dil k paas rahta hai,
(which always stays in our hearts,)
kabhi hansi ban kar,
(sometimes as laughter,)
kabhi aansuon mein,
(sometimes through tears,)
magar hamesha saath rehti hai.
(but always stays by our side.)

Yeh rishta dikhave ka mohtaaj nahi hota,
(This bond does not depend on show-off,)
khamosh rah kar bhi
(even without being spoken,)
sab kuch keh jaata hai,
(it says everything that matters,)
kitne hi matbhed kyun na ho,
(no matter how many differences arise,)
dil ke beech manbhed nahi hota.
(between hearts there is no real divide.)

Naseeb wala hota hai woh shaks,
(Truly fortunate is the one who)

jise zindagi mein
(in life)
sacchi dosti mil jaati hai.
(finds true friendship along the way.)

9. Hostel ke dost (Friends from hostel life)

Hostel mein reh kar maine ek naya ghar banaya,
(While living in a hostel, I built a new home,)
pehli baar ghar se door reh kar bhi
(for the first time, even away from my family,)
khud ko mehfooz paaya,
(I felt safe and secure,)
kuch naye dost bane, kuch naye tareeke seekhe.
(I made new friends, and learned new ways of living.)

Ek hi kamre mein hum sapne baant-te the,
(In the same room, we shared our dreams,)
raatein lambi hoti thi,
(nights felt long,)
baatein aur bhi zyada,
(conversations even longer,)
aur neend aksar din mein poori hoti thi.
(and sleep was often completed during the day.)
Zindagi ka matlab, kitabon se zyada
(and the meaning of life was understood more through friends)
doston se samajh aaya.
(than through books.)

Aaj sab apni-apni raahon mein hain,

(Today, we are all on our own paths,)

par woh saath, aur woh dosti----

(but that togetherness, and that friendship----)

zindagi bhar ke liye apne ho gaye.

(for a lifetime has become a part of us.)

10. Kuch dost peeche reh gaye (Some friends were left behind)

Kuch dost waqt ke saath peeche reh gaye,
(Some friends were left behind with time,)
na koi jhagda, na koi shikayat,
(there was no fight, no complaint,)
bas zindagi aage badh gayi.
(life simply moved ahead.)

Kabhi roz baat hoti thi,
(There was a time we spoke every day,)
ek din bhi call na karo to daant padti thi,
(missing even one call invited scolding,)
aaj sirf yaadon mein milte hain.
(today, we meet only in memories.)

Kabhi saath chalna aadat thi,
(Walking together was once a habit,)
aaj sirf message kar khairiyat pooch lete hain.
(today, we just message to ask if all is well.)

Na galat woh hain, na hum,
(Neither they are wrong, nor are we,)

bas raaste badal gaye,
(it's just that paths changed,)
shehar, zimmedaariyaan, aur sapne
(cities, responsibilities, and dreams)
dosti k beech mein aa gaye.
(came in between of friendship.)

11. Ek khas dost (A special friend)

Ek khaas dost hota hai,
(There is a special friend,)
jo har pal, dil ke paas rehta hai,
(who stays close to the heart at all times,)
na roz baat hoti hai,
(even if we don't talk every day,)
na saath rehna zaroori hota hai,
(and don't need to be together,)
phir bhi, apnapan kam nahi hota hai.
(the feeling of closeness never fades.)

Mahinon baat na ho,
(Even if months pass without conversation,)
phir bhi, koi doori mehsoos nahi hoti,
(no distance is truly felt,)
saalon milna na ho, phir bhi, dosti kamzor nahi hoti.
(even if years pass without meeting, the friendship does not grow weak.)

Hum samajh lete hain badhti zimmedaariyon ko,
(We understand the growing responsibilities of life,)
isliye, na gile hote hain, na shikwe,
(that's why there are no complaints or grudges,)

bas ek bharosa hota hai
(there is only a quiet trust)
jo waqt ke saath, aur gehra ho jaata hai.
(that deepens with time.)

12. Waqt nhi (No time)

Aaj har aish-o-aaraam logon ke daaman mein hai,
(Today, every comfort and luxury seems to be within people's reach,)
par dil khol kar hansne ke liye waqt nahi hai.
(yet to laugh freely from the heart there is no time.)

Din-raat daudti is duniya mein,
(In this world that runs day and night,)
jeene ke liye hi waqt nahi hai,
(there isn't even time to truly live,)
aankhon mein neend toh bahut hai,
(there is plenty of sleep in our eyes,)
par chain se sone ka waqt nahi hai.
(but to sleep peacefully there is no time.)

Anjaane log bahut mil jaate hain,
(We meet many strangers,)
par khaas dost ab koi nahi hai,
(but close friends are few and far between,)
tyohaar aaj bhi aate hain, par saath milkar
(festivals still arrive, but there is no one)
khushiyaan baantne wala koi nahi hai.
(to sit together and share happiness.)

Dil ghamon se bhara hua hai,

(The heart is filled with unspoken sorrow,)

par ae zindagi,

(yet, oh life,)

is bheed mein logon ke paas

(in this crowded world people)

rone ka bhi waqt nahi hai.

(don't even have time to cry.)

13. Wo jo peeche reh gya (What was left behind)

Shehar ki bheed mein
(In the crowded rush of the city,)
hum bas bhaagte hi kyun rehte hain,
(why do we keep running all the time?)
paisa, shohrat sab yaad rehta hai,
(Money and fame are always remembered,)
par maa ki godi mein sar rakh kar
(but resting our head in a mother's lap)
baatein karna kyun bhool jaate hain.
(and sharing quiet conversations is what we forget.)

Sawan ki pehli baarish mein
(In the first rain of the monsoon,)
boondon ka shor toh yaad rehta hai,
(we remember the sound of raindrops, clearly,)
par usi baarish mein
(but in that same rain,)
mitti ki woh saundhi khushboo
(the earthy, fragrant scent of wet soil)
mehsoos karna kyun bhool jaate hain.
(to truly feel it is what we forget.)

Agar yahi hai jeena,
(If this is what living means,)
agar yahi hai kuch haasil karna,
(if this is what we call achievement,)
toh phir, ek nanhe bachche ki hansi dekh kar
(then why is it that on seeing a little child's laughter,)
aankhon mein aansoo kyun aa jaate hain.
(our eyes fill with tears without warning?)

14. Zindagi, thoda thahar (Life, pause for a while)

Ae zindagi, zara thahar,
(Life, pause for a moment,)
kuch pal ke liye, ek gehri saans toh le,
(take a deep breath,)
zindagi kat rahi hai, daudte waqt ki tarah,
(life is passing by like rushing time,)
zara ruk kar, kuch palon ko mehsoos to kar.
(slow down and allow a few moments to be felt.)

Jeete toh sabhi hain,
(Everyone lives,)
par kuch pal
(but for a few moments,)
dil se laga kar dekh,
(try living from the heart,)
har kadam par
(at every step,)
khud ko ghisne se behtar hai
(instead of wearing yourself down,)
kabhi apnon ke saath
(sometimes with your loved ones,)
khud ko baant kar to dekh.
(try sharing yourself.)

15. Adhura rah jata hai (Left incomplete)

Kuch sawaal, kuch ehsaas
(Some questions, some feelings)
adhure reh jaate hain,
(remain incomplete,)
barson beet jaate hain,
(years pass by,)
par kuch armaan, adhure reh jaate hain.
(yet some desires are never fulfilled.)

Kabhi yeh, kabhi woh karte-karte,
(Busy with one thing and then another, while constantly doing,)
khud ke sapne peeche reh jaate hain,
(our own dreams get left behind,)
"Aaj nahi, kal,"
("not today, tomorrow,")
kehte-kehte, khayalat adhure reh jaate hai.
(we keep saying and thoughts left behind.)

Ruk zara, ek saans toh le,
(Pause for a moment, take a breath,)
warna yeh pal beet jaayenge,
(or else these moments will quietly slip away,)

thoda waqt nikaal,

(take out a little time,)

khud ko samet kar dekh,

(try to gather yourself,)

varna zindagi poori hote-hote bhi

(otherwise life, even while appearing complete,)

adhuri reh jaayegi.

(will remain unfinished.)

16. Kati patang (A cut kite)

Kati patang ki tarah kho jaate hain kuch log,
(Like a cut kite,some people drift away,)
yaad rakh kar bhi, bhool jaate hain kuch log.
(even while remembering us, they forget, some people.)

Kabhi har pal saath-saath raha karte the,
(There was a time when we were together at every moment,)
khushi ho ya gham, sab humse baant liya karte the,
(whether in joy or sorrow, they shared everything with us,)
aaj yaad kar ke bhi bhool jaate hain,
(today, even when they remember, they tend to forget,)
na jaane kaise yun badal jaate hain kuch log.
(no one knows how some people change so completely.)

Jeene ke sahaare aur bhi hote hain,
(There are many supports to keep living,)
phir bhi, na jaane kyun
(yet for some reason)
zarurat ban jaate hain kuch log.
(some people become a necessity in our lives.)

Aur phir samajh aata hai ----

(And then we understand ----)

kuch log humein chhodne ke liye nahi,

(some people do not come to leave us,)

sirf yaad banne ke liye aate hain.

(they come only to become memories.)

17. Khuda se kya mange (What more I can ask from God)

Ae Khuda, tu hi bata,
(O God, you tell me,)
ab hum tujh se kya maange.
(what more can I ask of you now.)

Hamdum ka pyaar aur saath hai,
(there is the love and companionship of a soulmate,)
toh bhala duaon mein aur kya maange.
(so what else could I possibly ask for in my prayers.)

Jiski har dua bin maange qubool hui ho,
(When every unasked prayer has already been answered,)
woh insaan khuda se aur kya maange.
(what more can one ask of God.)

Jab shikwa, sikayat se pehle hi door ho jaaye,
(When every complaint is resolved even before it is spoken,)
toh mandiron mein haath utha kar kya maange.
*(then what is left to ask for with folded hands in

temples.)

Apne hamdum ke pyaar aur saath se
(With the love and presence of my companion,)
zindagi roshan hai,
(life feels full of light,)
ab in khushiyon ke baad
(after being blessed with such happiness,)
armaanon se aur kya maange.
(what more can I ask of my desires.)

18. Pyaar ka ahsas (The feeling of love)

Dil ka bina wajah
(The heart without any reason)
halka ho jaana,
(suddenly feels light,)
baithe-baithe yun hi
(sitting quietly, without effort,)
uske khayalon mein kho jaana.
(getting lost in their thoughts.)

Har pal uske hone ka ehsaas rehna,
(At every moment, the feeling of their presence stays close,)
na lafzon ki zarurat,
(no words are needed,)
bas aankhon se
(just through the eyes)
har haal bayan ho jaana.
(every emotion is understood.)

Ghanton baatein karne ke baad bhi
(Even after hours of conversation,)
kuch kehna baaki reh jaana,
(something still remains unsaid,)

yeh jo adhoora sa ahsas hai -----
(this incompleteness feeling----)
shayad, yeh hi pyaar hai.
(perhaps this is love.)

19. Intezzar (Waiting)

Pyaar ka koi mausam nahi hota,
(Love has no season,)
dilbar ko yaad karne ka
(there is no fixed time)
koi samay nahi hota.
(to miss the one you love.)

Koi dekhe toh hamari bebasi,
(If someone were to look closely,)
ek-dooje se milne ki chah mein
(in the longing to meet each other,)
hum chup-chaap tadapte rehte hain,
(we quietly continue to ache,)
par is zamaane ko
(but this world)
zara bhi taras nahi aata.
(does not feel even a little compassion.)

Kab se dilbar se milne ka intezaar hai humein,
(For so long, we have been waiting to meet our beloved,)
par na jaane kyun
(yet somehow,)
khuda ko yeh mauka manzoor nahi hota.
(God has not found it right to grant this moment.)

20. Khamoshi mein mohabbat (Love within silence)

Jab tum khud ko
(When you find yourself)
baarish ki boondon mein khamoshi se ghira paoge,
(even among falling rain surrounded by silence,)
jab neele aasman tale, dil ko bhari saans lete paoge.
(when beneath the blue sky your heart feels heavy with every breath.)

Jab hansi ke shor mein bhi, khud ko andar se khaali lagoge,
(When even within loud laughter you feel empty inside,)
jab apni baatein daba kar sirf muskura kar chal jaoge.
(when you bury your words and walk away with a smile.)

Dil chupchaap kahega ek naam baar-baar,
(Your heart will quietly whisper one name again and again,)
jo tum keh nahi paoge,
(that you won't dare to speak aloud,)

Us pal jaan lena....
(In that moment, know this....)
khamoshi ke beech hi mohabbat apni jagah bana rhi hai,
(within that silence itself love will find its place,)
aur dheere dheere
(and slowly)
dil kisi ke saath chalna seekh rha hai.
(your heart is learning to walk with someone.)

21. Tum ho to (When you are with me)

Tum ho to main hoon,
(When you are with me, I truly exist,)
Tumhare bina, mera na koi wajood hai,
(without you, I have no sense of being.)

Tum sath ho,
(When you are by my side,)
to khushiyon ki bahaar hai
(life feels like a season of happiness.)
Tum ho to,
(When you are here,)
har lamha ek nayi jhankaar hai
(every moment feels like a new melody.)

Meri duniya tumse hain roshan,
(My world shines because of you,)
Tumse hi sajeed hai
(it is filled and made beautiful by you.)
Tum ho to main hoon,
(When you are with me, I am complete,)
Tere sang jeevan ha har pal, khud me ek jeevan h
(with you, every moment of life feels like a life in itself.)

22. Tumhaare saath Chalna (Walking beside you)

Tumhaare saath chalne se
(Walking beside you,)
raahen aasaan lagti hain,
(the paths feel easier,)
mera haath jab tumhaare haathon mein ho,
(when my hand rests in yours,)
toh har manzil kareeb lagti hai.
(every destination feels close.)

Na jaane kya khaas baat hai tum mein,
(I don't know what is so special about you,)
par tumhaare saath chalne par
(but when I walk with you,)
zindagi thodi aur khubsoorat lagti hai.
(life feels a little more beautiful.)

23. Roothe jo khuda (When life turns away)

Roothe jo khuda,
(Even if God turns away,)
toh mana lenge hum,
(I will gently win him back,)
kitne bhi ho jamane ke sitam,
(no matter how many hardships the world brings,)
unhein apna lenge hum.
(I will accept them as mine.)

Agar tum saath ho mere,
(If you are by my side,)
toh gehare tufaan mein bhi,
(then even in the fiercest storms,)
khud ko sambhal lenge hum.
(I will hold myself strong.)

Hai bharosa apni chahat par,
(I have faith in our love,)
har mushkil pal ko
(that we will face every difficult moment)
hanste-hanste seh lenge hum.
(with a smile.)

Jab saath ho apne humdum ka,

(When my companion is with me,)

toh zindagi sirf kaatenge nahi,

(I will not merely pass through life,)

har pal me nya jeevan jee lenge hum.

(I will live every moment like a new life.)

24. Humsafar (Life's companion)

Hamare jeevan ka safar,
(The journey of our life)
humsafar ki rooh se juda hota hai,
(is connected to the soul of our companion.)

Agar koi saath ho
(when someone walks beside us,)
jo muskuraye aur raahen dikhaye.
(smiling and showing the way,)
Jab kabhi gham ho,
(When sorrow comes,)
toh dil ko sambhaale,
(they comfort the heart,)
roothe toh manaaye,
(when we are upset, they gently make things right,)
aur safar ke har mod par,
(and at every turn of life,)
jjannat ka ehsaas karaaye.
(make it feel like heaven.)

Khush kismat hain hum,
(We are truly fortunate)
jo yeh saath mila,

(to have this companionship,)
sajda karte hain hum us rab ka,
(and bow in gratitude to God,)
jisne hum pe yeh reham barsaya.
(who blessed us with such a beautiful feeling.)

25. Ek khaas din (A special day)

Aaj ka din bahut khaas hai,
(Today is a very special day,)
mera sanam mere saath hai,
(my beloved is by my side,)
kuch beete lamhon ki yaadein hain,
(there are memories of moments gone by,)
toh kuch unkahi si baatein hain.
(and some unspoken feelings too.)

Kuch anmol ehsaas hain,
(There are priceless emotions,)
toh kuch kimti khwaab hain,
(and some precious dreams,)
jo pal humne saath bitaaye,
(the moments we spent together,)
har woh pal gham se azaad hain.
(each one free from sorrow.)

Kuch waqt ho gaya hamare rishte ki shuruaat ko,
(Some time has passed since our relationship began,)
woh pehli mulaakaat ko,
(since our first meeting,)

kabhi dost, toh kabhi apni jaan kehte the,
(sometimes we called each other friends, sometimes our beloved,)
tumhari ek muskaan ke liye hum betaab rehte the.
(longing just to see your smile.)

Tumhaara pyaar mere jeene ka sahaara hai,
(Your love is my strength to live,)
mere paas aur kuch nahi,
(I have nothing else,)
bas tumhaari wafa ka ek pyaara sa tohfa hai.
(only the precious gift of your loyalty.)

26. Fariyaad (A prayer)

Khuda se aaj kuch fariyaad karte hain,
(Today, I make a humble prayer to God,)
tum hamesha salaamat raho---- yehi ardaas karte hain.
(asking that you always remain safe and well.)

Tumhaari aankhen kabhi nam na hon,
(May your eyes never fill with tears,)
jo tumhe udaas kare,
(may no sorrow)
aisa koi gham na ho.
(ever make you sad.)

Tumhaari har mushkil humse hokar guzre,
(May every hardship pass through me first,)
chahe kitne bhi dard hon,
(no matter how much pain there is,)
unki chhaaya tum tak na pahunche.
(may it never reach you.)

Tum dil mein rehte ho hamare,
(You live in my heart,)
yeh silsila kabhi na toote,
(may this bond never break,)

hum har kadam tumhaare saath rahein---
(may I walk beside you at every step,)
bas itni si dua karte hain.
(that is my only prayer.)

27. Jeene ki wajah (The reason to live)

Na jaane kab se tum,
(I don't know since when)
hamare jeene ki wajah ban gaye,
(you became the reason for my life,)
tumne hum par itna pyaar lutaaya,
(you showered me with so much love,)
ki dil-o-dimaag mein bas tum hi chha gaye.
(that you filled my heart and mind completely.)

Bin bole hi
(Without a single word,)
tumne har baat samjhi hai,
(you understood everything,)
achha ho ya bura,
(whether good or bad,)
har pal dil ke paas rakha hai.
(you kept me close to your heart in every moment.)

Yeh jo zindagi mein itni mithaas hai,
(The sweetness in my life,)
yeh tumhaare sacche pyaar ka hi tohfa hai.
(is a gift of your true love.)

Ab dua mein bas yehi fariyaad karte hain----

(Now my only prayer is----)

khuda salaamat rakhe tumhe,

(may God always keep you safe,)

kyunki tum par hum dil-o-jaan nisaar karte hain.

(because I devote my heart and soul to you.)

28. Tanhai (Loneliness)

Ae Khuda,
(O God,)
hamari tarah
(do not give them)
unhein tanhaayi na dena,
(loneliness like mine,)
hum jee lenge tanha,
(I will live through this solitude,)
magar unhein
(but please do not give them)
koi judaai na dena.
(the pain of separation.)

Hamari nigahon mein
(In my eyes,)
ab bhi
(even now,)
unki soorat basi rahe,
(their face continues to live,)
woh bhale hi humein
(even if I may no longer)
kabhi dikhai na den.
(be able to see them again.)

29. Bewafaai (Betrayal)

Ek bewafa aakar humein
(A faithless one came to me)
pyaar ka matlab samjha rahi thi,
(teaching me the meaning of love,)
kisi aur ki baahon mein reh kar
(while resting in someone else's arms,)
wafa ka paath padha rahi thi.
(giving lessons about loyalty.)

Yeh jaante hue bhi
(Even knowing)
ki humein unse mohabbat hai,
(that I loved her deeply,)
woh humein, kisi aur ki kahaani suna rahi thi.
(she still told me stories of someone else.)

Ae Khuda, yeh kaisa saleeka hai,
(O God, what kind of fate is this,)
khud ko dekhe bina
(without looking at herself,)
woh humein, hamari hi nazron mein gira rahi thi.
(she was making me fall in my own eyes.)

30. Khamoshi ke baad (After the silence)

Jab baatein kam hone lagi,
(When conversations started to fade,)
aur sawaal zyada hone lage,
(and questions began to grow,)
tab samajh aaya kuch badal raha hai.
(that's when I understood something was changing.)

Pehle shor tha,
(First there was noise,)
phir bahas hui,
(then there were arguments,)
aur phir ek din
(and then one day)
bas khamoshi reh gayi.
(only silence remained.)

Na koi shikwa, na koi jawaab,
(No complaints, no answers,)
bas doori ka ehsaas reh gaya.
(just the feeling of distance was left behind.)

Khamoshi ke baad yeh samajh aaya----
(After the silence, I realized----)

kuch rishte toot-te nahi hain,

(some relationships do not break suddenly,)

bas dhund ki tarah

(they simply fade away)

dheere-dheere

(slowly,)

kho jaate hain.

(like mist.)

31. Adhura pyaar (Incomplete love)

Har pyaar apne mukaam tak pahunche,
(Not every love reaches its destined place,)
yeh zaroori toh nahi,
(this is not always necessary,)
har mehboob ko
(not every lover)
uski mehbooba ka saath mile,
(gets to walk life with their beloved,)
yeh bhi zaroori toh nahi.
(this too is not guaranteed.)

Kuch rishte
(Some relationships)
bas kuch waqt ke liye hi bante hain,
(are meant only for a short time,)
jinmein pyaar bhi hota hai, vishwas bhi hota hai,
(where love exists, trust exists,)
saath jeene-mar ne ka junoon bhi hota hai.
(and even the passion to live and die together,)

Har pyaar karne wale ko
(Not everyone who loves)
zindagi bhar ka saath mile,

(is blessed with lifelong companionship,)

yeh zaroori nahi hota,

(this is not always meant to be,)

saccha hota hai pyaar,

(love may be true,)

phir bhi aksar adhoora reh jaata hai.

(yet it often remains incomplete.)

32. Khud se milna (Finding myself again)

Toot kar bhi hum bikhre nahi,
(Even after breaking, I did not fall apart,)
dard mila, par hum haare nahi.
(pain came, but I did not lose.)

Kuch pal roye, kuch yaadein sambhaali,
(I cried for a while, held on to some memories,)
phir dheere-dheere
(and then slowly,)
khud se hi dosti kar li.
(I made peace with myself.)

Jis pyaar mein khud ko kho diya tha,
(In the love where I had lost myself,)
ab usi zindagi mein
(in that very life)
khud ko dhoond liya.
(I found myself again.)

Samajh aaya----
(I realized----)
khush rehne ke liye
(to be happy)

kisi aur ka saath nahi,

(I do not always need someone else,)

kabhi-kabhi

(sometimes)

khud ka saath hi kaafi hota hai.

(my own company is enough.)

33. Beti – Khuda ki rehmat (Daughter - a blessing)

Ek pyaari si muskaan hai woh,
(She is a sweet little smile,)
mere hothon par saja har raag hai woh,
(the melody that rests on my lips,)
phool kahun ya kali use,
(whether I call her a flower or a bud,)
mere jeevan ka aadhaar hai woh.
(she is the foundation of my life.)

Uski paayal ki chhankaar
(The sound of her anklets)
se ghar mein sangeet hai,
(fills the home with music,)
aur uski meethi si hansi se
(and her sweet laughter)
har pal jaise koi tyohaar hai.
(turns every moment into a celebration.)

Papa ki aankhon ki raunak hai woh,
(She is the sparkle in her father's eyes,)
aur maa ka guroor hai woh.
(and the pride of her mother.)

Koi aur nahi,
(She is no one else)
meri jaan, meri apni beti hai woh,
(but my precious daughter,)
is kudrat ka ek anmol uphaar hai woh.
(an invaluable gift from nature.)

34. Beti - Ek dua (Daughter – a prayer)

Khuda ki rehmat ka ek nagma hai tu,
(You are a melody of God's blessings,)
hamare jeevan ka anmol gehna hai tu.
(you are the most precious jewel of our lives.)

Teri hansi se ghar mein raunak chha jaaye,
(Your laughter fills our home with joy,)
tere masoom sawaalon se
(and your innocent questions)
hamare hothon par muskaan aa jaaye.
(bring smiles to our faces.)

Tu sabke dilon par yun hi raaj kare,
(May you always rule hearts with love,)
shohrat se zyada
(more than fame)
apnon ka khayaal kare.
(value your loved ones.)

Rab se har pal yehi dua karti hoon,
(I pray to God every moment,)
tu pankh laga kar udti rahe,
(that you keep flying with your wings spread wide,)

poore hon woh saare sapne,
(that all your dreams come true,)
jin se tere dil ko sukoon mile.
(and bring peace to your heart.)

35. Beti ka aagman (The arrival of a daughter)

Suraj dada ne khul kar roshni phailaayi,
(The sun spread its light freely,)
bhavron ne madhur sangeet sunaaya,
(the bees played sweet melodies,)
har panchhi aur phoolon ne hans kar raag sajaaya,
(every bird and flower joyfully joined the song,)
mubarak ho --- aaj ghar mein beti ka aagman hua.
(congratulations--- today a daughter arrived in our home.)

Yeh din bahut khaas hai,
(This day is very special,)
ek chhoti si gudiya aaj ghar aayi hai,
(a little doll has come home today,)
aur zindagi mein nayi roshni laayi hai.
(bringing new light into our lives.)

Khuda se fariyaad hai ki teri har ichha poori ho,
(We pray to God that every wish of yours comes true,)
hum toh har pal tere saath rahenge,
(we will always be by your side,)
par tujhme apni sharton par jeene ki taakat ho.
(but may you also have the courage to live life on your

own terms.)

Tere jeevan ke raaste mein kaante thode kam hon,
(May there be fewer thorns on your path of life,)
chehre par har pal muskaan ho,
(may your face always carry a smile,)
dil se yeh hi dua hai ki teri zindagi mein
(our heartfelt prayer is that in your life)
har din khushiyon ki bauchhaar ho.
(every day showers happiness.)

36. Waqt (Time)

Waqt na rukta hai,
(Time does not stop,)
na kisi ka intezaar karta hai,
(it waits for no one,)
bas dheere-dheere sab kuch badal deta hai.
(it slowly changes everything.)

Jo kal apna tha,
(What once was ours,)
aaj yaad ban jaata hai,
(becomes a memory today,)
jo aaj paas hai,
(what is close today,)
kal door ho jaata hai.
(may be far tomorrow.)

Waqt ne humein rona bhi sikhaaya,
(Time taught us how to cry,)
aur muskurana bhi,
(and also how to smile,)
tootna bhi sikhaaya,
(it taught us how to break,)
aur phir sambhalna bhi.
(and then how to heal.)

Ab ja k Samajh aaya---
(Now, I realized---)
waqt kuch cheenta nahi,
(time does not take anything away,)
bas humein jeena sikhaata hai.
(it simply teaches us how to live.)

37. Sukoon (Peace)

Sukoon kisi manzil ka naam nahi,
(Peace is not the name of a destination,
yeh toh bas thehar jaane ka ehsaas hai.
(it is simply the feeling of pausing.)

Kabhi muskaan mein milta hai,
(Sometimes it is found in a smile,)
kabhi aansuon ke baad,
(sometimes after tears,)
kabhi apnon ke saath,
(sometimes with loved ones,)
to kabhi ek bacche ki hansi me.
(and sometimes in a child's smile.)

Zindagi ke shor ke beech
(Amid the noise of life,)
jab dil shant ho jaaye,
(when the heart becomes still,)
aur saans halki ho jaaye---
(and the breath feels light---)

shayad usi pal ka naam sukoon hai.
(perhaps that moment is what we call peace.)

38. Shukriya zindagi (Thank you, life)

Shukriya zindagi,
(Thank you, life,)
jo diya, uske liye bhi,
(for everything you gave me,)
aur jo chheen liya, uske liye bhi.
(and even for what you took away.)

Khushiyon ke palon ke liye,
(For moments of happiness,)
aur aansuon ke sabak ke liye,
(and for the lessons hidden in tears,)
hasne ke maukon ke liye,
(for chances to laugh,)
aur sambhalna sikhaane ke liye.
(and for teaching me how to rise again.)

Kyunki,
(Because)
har mod par
(at every turn,)
kuch na kuch sikhaaya,
(you taught me something,)

Aur aaj jo hoon main,
(and who I am today is)
uski wajah tum hi ho.
(because of you.)

39. Nayi subah (A new morning)

Har raat ke baad ek subah hoti hai,
(After every night, a morning comes,)
har andhere ke baad roshni hoti hai.
(after every darkness, there is light.)

Jo kal toot gaya, aaj sambhal sakta hai,
(What broke yesterday can heal today,)
jo aaj ro raha hai, kal muskurana seekh sakta hai.
(the one who cries today can learn to smile tomorrow.)

Waqt dheere dheere zakhmon ko bhar deta hai,
(Time slowly heals wounds,)
aur dil ko phir se sapne de deta hai.
(and fills the heart with dreams again.)

Bas bharosa rakho
(Just keep faith)
zindagi har roz naya mauka deti hai.
(life gives a new chance every day.)

40. Chhod dena (Letting go)

Kabhi kabhi,

(Sometimes)

pakad kar rakhna thaka deta hai,

(holding on becomes tiring,)

aur chhod dena hi

(and letting go itself)

sukoon ban jaata hai.

(becomes peace.)

Jo saath chala,

(Those who walked with you,)

use dil mein sambhaal lo,

(keep them in your heart,)

jo peeche reh gaya,

(and those left behind,)

use yaadon mein chhod do.

(leave them in memories.)

Har dard ko saath le kar, aage badhna zaroori nahi,

(It is not necessary to carry every pain forward,)

kuch bojh dil se utaar dena hi behtar hota hai.

(some burdens are better laid down.)

Chhod dena matlab haarna nahi,

(Letting go does not mean losing,)

kabhi kabhi,

(sometimes,)

yeh hi toh nayi shuruaat hoti hai.

(it is the beginning of something new.)

41. Chhoti chhoti khushiyaan (Little joys)

Subah ki pehli dhoop ka chhoona,
(The gentle touch of the first morning sunlight,)
aangan mein baith kar subah ki chai ki garam chuski lena.
(sitting in the courtyard and sipping warm morning tea.)

Kisi apne ki muskaan bhari baat sunna,
(Listening to a loved one's smile-filled words,)
kisi bachche ki khilti hui hansi kaanon mein padna,
(hearing a child's blooming laughter,)
kabhi maa ki paayal ki chhankaar sunna.
(and sometimes the sound of a mother's anklets.)

Bina wajah hothon par aayi hui hansi,
(A smile that appears without any reason,)
khidki par girti pehli baarish ki boondein,
(the first raindrops falling on the window,)
purane gaane dheere dheere bajte hue,
(old songs playing softly,)
ya apnon ke saath baith kar chhote chhote khel khelna.
or sitting with loved ones and playing little games together.)

Zindagi koi badi cheez nahi,

(Life is not something grand,)

yeh toh bas in chhoti chhoti khushiyon ka khazaana hai.

(it is simply a treasure of these little joys.)

42. Papa ki khamoshi (A father's silence)

Papa zyada baatein nahi karte,
(Father doesn't speak much,)
par har baat samajh jaate hain.
(yet he understands everything.)

Apni thakaan chhupa kar,
(Hiding his own tiredness,)
hamari muskaan ke liye roz nikal jaate hain.
(he steps out every day for our smiles.)

Kabhi dard bhi ho to chehre par shikayat nahi hoti,
(Even when he is in pain, there is no complaint on his face,)
bas khamoshi mein hi unki mohabbat bol jaati hai.
(his love speaks quietly through his silence.)

Hamari zarooraton ke aage apni khwahishen rakhna unhone kabhi seekha hi nahi,
(He never learned to place his wishes before our needs,)
isliye shayad woh kam bolte hain, par zyada nibhaate hain.
(perhaps that is why he speaks less, but gives more.)

Papa ki khamoshi mein poori duniya chhupi hoti hai,
(Within a father's silence lies an entire world,)
jo bina kahe hi sab kuch de jaati hai.
(that gives everything without a word.)

www.ingramcontent.com/pod-product-compliance
Lightning Source LLC
Chambersburg PA
CBHW070645240926
51846CB00003BA/783
* 9 7 8 9 3 7 5 2 7 2 6 0 1 *